Dr. A.P.J. Abdul Kalam

Regarded as an ideal Indian and a source of inspiration for the future generations, President Dr. A.P.J. Abdul Kalam was born on October 15, 1931 in an ordinary Tamil family of Rameshwaram in Tamil Nadu. His full name is Abul Pakir Jainulabedin Abdul Kalam. His father Jainulabedin and mother Aashiamma were a simple and religious-minded couple. They held an honourable place in the society and were regarded as an ideal couple. They lived in a joint family.

Kalam's father was a simple person. He never cared for luxuries and gave more importance to rational thoughts and human values. The senior-most priest of Rameshwaram temple, Pt. Lakshman Shastri was his dear friend. They used to have long spiritual discussions and Kalam as a boy listened attentively to those discussions. Although Kalam could not understand everything but his thinking has been largely influenced by it.

During his childhood, Abdul Kalam partook his meals with his mother sitting on the kitchen floor. His mother used to spread a banana leaf before him and serve him a simple meal of garnished rice, tasty *sambhar*, home made pickles and fresh coconut *chutney*.

Right from his childhood Dr. Kalam was honest, God fearing, labourious and simple, traits which he inherited from his parents.

Dr. Kalam's childhood was deeply influenced by his cousin Shamsuddin who was the sole distributor of newspapers in Rameshwaram. During those days there was great demand for *Dinamani,* a Tamil newspaper. Though Kalam had not yet learnt to read yet he satisfied himself by looking at the pictures, when Shamsuddin used to bring the newspaper.

When Second World War started in 1939, Kalam was only 8 years old. During those days, there was a sudden increase in demand for tamarind seeds in the market. Although Kalam did not know the reason, he started collecting tamarind seeds and selling them at grocery shops. This way he earned one anna everyday.

During that time emergency was announced in India because of the Second World War. As a result, the trains did not stop at Rameshwaram station. In that situation bundles of newspapers were thrown from the moving train between Rameshwaram and Dhanushkodi station. At that time Shamsuddin felt the need of an assistant who could assist him in picking up those bundles. Child Kalam was well prepared to help him and in this way he earned his first salary from his cousin Shamsuddin.

In his childhood, Kalam used to wear a skull cap, which is a symbol of being a Muslim. At that time Kalam was a student of class V in a primary school. Once a new teacher came to his class. Kalam was sitting in the front row with his friend Ramanand Shastri. The new teacher did not like a Hindu boy

sitting next to a Muslim boy. So he ordered Kalam to sit at the last bench. Child Kalam did not like this. Ramanand Shastri too was very much grieved by this behaviour of the teacher.

When Lakshman Shastri, Ramanand Shastri's father came to know about it he called the teacher and reprimanded him, "You should not sow the seeds of religious discrimination in the hearts of innocent children."

The teacher apologized for his behaviour and eventually a great change came in his attitude.

Having completed the primary education, Kalam was admitted to Swartz High School in Ramanathapuram. He had to stay in the school hostel. While at Ramanathapuram he very often missed his parents, his home and especially the South Indian sweetmeat 'poli' prepared by his mother.

In spite of his great love for home, Kalam was fully dedicated to his studies because his parents and teachers had high expectations from him. He worked very hard to achieve his aim and nothing could deter him from his firm determination.

Once, during his school days, it so happened that the maths teacher Ramakrishna Aiyyar was teaching in another class. Unknowingly Kalam entered the class room. Seeing this, the teacher immediately caught hold off him by his neck and hit him with a rod before the entire class. Later, when Kalam secured the highest marks in mathematics, Ramakrishna Aiyyar narrated the episode at the time of morning prayer before everyone. He announced, "The boy whom I beat with a rod, will become a great man one day. Mark my words, this

student is going to become the pride of his school and teachers."

Since childhood, Kalam developed a deep liking for the mysteries of the sky, and the flight of birds across the seas. He enjoyed the sight of cranes flying over the sea and long flights of birds. He decided that one day he too would go for long flights in the sky. Later he was the first person in Rameshwaram to fly in a plane.

When Kalam completed his schooling, he was brimming with enthusiasm and confidence. Without a second thought he entered Saint Joseph College, Tiruchirapalli, in 1950. During his college days he worked hard. He was a very disciplined student. When he was a final year student in the college he developed a great liking for English Literature. He read all the available books on English literature by great writers such as Tolstoy, Scott, Hardy, etc. Also when he was a student of the final year he developed a deep inclination towards Physics. He felt great pleasure in reading about the highest knowledge of astronomy, particularly our solar system.

To fulfill his dream, Kalam decided to study Engineering after his B.Sc. from Saint Joseph College. For this, he needed at least one thousand rupees, but his father did not have that much money. It was his elder sister Johra who came to his rescue. She mortgaged her gold bangles and necklace and got Kalam admitted to Madras Institute of Technology (MIT). At that time Kalam had a single ambition – to be a pilot.

Modesty is a good quality but Kalam had to face many

भौतिकी

difficulties at MIT because of it. Because of his humble nature, he was quite hesitant to ask questions or reply to them in front of everyone in the class. That is why, his fellow students used to make fun of him. Kalam was depressed about it. He lost his self-confidence. During those days, he used to remember his father's teachings and inspirational advices. His father often said: "One who understands others, learns; but a person is called wise when he understands himself. Learning without wisdom is nothing but crammed knowledge, it is of no use. Knowing oneself is much important." This thought brought self-confidence in him and he was recharged with enthusiasm for achieving his aim. During his studies in MIT, Kalam was inspired by three teachers – Prof. Spander, Prof. K.A. B. Panadalaiin and Prof. Narsingha Rao to give his thoughts a concrete form. Kalam was able to construct his work field with the joint assistance of these teachers which laid the foundation of his life.

After completing his third year from Madras Institute of Technology, he joined as a technical instructor at the Hindustan Aeronautics Ltd. After becoming an aeronautical engineer from Hindustan Aeronautics Ltd. he got two excellent job opportunities and both of which were enough to fulfil his childhood dreams. One was in the Indian Air Force and the other was in the Technical Development and Production Directorate, Ministry of Defence. Kalam prepared well with full dedication and hard labour. He was very much assured of his selection in the Indian Air Force.

But he was deeply disappointed when he came to know that out of 25 candidates, only 8 had been selected and he had stood ninth. It was a great setback. He was disappointed but he soon recovered from this. Another chance yet remained with him. Here he achieved success and was appointed as Technical Assistant in the Technical Development and Production Directorate, Ministry of Defence, Govt. of India.

In the 1960s, Dr. Kalam joined the Vikram Sarabhai Space Centre, Thumba (Kerala). There he played a key role in the development of the first indigenous satellite launcher. After that in 1982, he worked as Director of the Defence Research and the Development Organisation of India and was in charge of the Joint Controlled Launcher Development Programme. After that he worked as a Scientific Advisor to the Defence Minister and later as a Defence Advisor to the Prime Minister. He also played a major role in the 1998 nuclear experiments. Dr. Kalam was quite co-operative with his colleagues in the work front. He paid attention to their ideas. He never made an attempt to impose his ideas upon them. He tried to maintain discipline, faith and mutual understanding in his team. His behaviour was friendly with everyone. Because of these qualities, Kalam was a favourite among his colleagues. In spite of these, he has few friends in his private life. He has been totally dedicated to his work throughout his life and work has been his companion.

While serving the country in various ways, Dr. Kalam not only fulfilled the dreams of his parents and teachers but also his own. He put India in an equal position with advanced countries

and thereby enhanced its honour and pride.

After retirement, Dr. Kalam taught at the Annamalai University in Tamil Nadu. He has been conferred with various prestigious awards. In 1981 he was awarded the 'Padma Bhushan'; in 1990, 'Padma Vibhushan', and in 1997, he was honoured with the 'Bharat Ratna', the highest civilian award. Besides this, he was awarded the Dr. Virender Roy Space Award, National Nehru Award and Arya Bhatt Award. Twenty-eight universities throughout the country awarded him the title of Doctor of Science.

Undoubtedly we can assume Dr. Kalam as a fortunate person after having received so many awards and honours but he did not get anything out of luck but as a result of sheer hard work and strong determination. He had to face obstacles throughout his life at every step. There was problem of economic scarcity, lack of will power, non-cooperation of colleagues, and bitterness, failures, ironical comments and many other things, but nothing could deter him from the path. On account of this, Dr. Kalam developed more modesty in his behaviour after every achievement.

Whether it was the assignment as a scientist or as a teacher, whatever work he was given, he accomplished it sincerely.

During his tenure as a teacher in Annamalai University, Dr. Kalam was nominated as the President of India. On 25th July 2002, he was elected the 12th President of India. He took oath as a president under Chief Justice B.N. Kripal.

As President, Dr. Kalam replied strictly to the criticism of those people who were protesting strongly against a scientist being appointed as President, who had the image of a 'missile man'. Dr. Kalam's heart is as soft as a child's although he has firm determination and will power in achieving his aim. He forgets himself in the company of children and becomes a part of them. He regards children as a seed in which the future tree is hidden. He is of the view that children are the future of India. He has not only hopes from the young generation, but also has full faith in them. He has the dream of educating each and every child of India and it is his message that we should nurture high dreams and at the same time create confidence in our heart to transform those dreams into reality, because this thought only can take our country towards path of progress.

Dr. Kalam believes that by 2020, our country will be able to become a developed country. To transform his ideas into a solid form, Dr. Kalam has many plans. These programmes can turn to a reality, but it is not possible only by the inspiration of a few selected Indians, for that, every Indian has to work together. He accepts that the role of the younger generation is of utmost importance in the development of a nation. Therefore he considers the Indian youth as the most powerful resource and inspires them to work unitedly. He opines that if you are a good man, then you can perform every job in the best manner. For example, if we take the instance of Dr. Kalam's personality then he is a capable scientist, an ideal teacher besides being a wonderful colleague and an excellent writer. He has not only a

good knowledge of Indian classical music, but he is a perfect violin player too. He also has interest in gardening. He feels unlimited peace of mind and pleasure in the company of nature. He has a very busy work schedule, but even then he has kept a few regular habits such as morning walk, prayer, yoga, head massage with coconut oil before bath and drinking a glass of milk before retiring at night.

He always says that keep every moment busy and meaningful, but at the same time, always take out time to feel the fragrance of flowers or to watch the myriad colours of butterflies.

Dr. Kalam has this message for the young generation –

As a young citizen of India,
armed with technology, knowledge and love for my nation,
I realise, small aim is a crime.
I will work and sweat for a great vision,
the vision of transforming India into a developed nation
powered by economic strength with value system.
I am one of the citizens of a billion,
only the vision will ignite the billion souls.
It has entered into me,
the ignited souls compared to any resource,
is the most powerful resource
on the earth, above the earth and under the earth.
I will keep the lamp of knowledge burning
to achieve the vision—Developed India.

□□□